Bil Keane

FAWCETT GOLD MEDAL • NEW YORK

A Fawcett Gold Medal Book
Published by Ballantine Books
Copyright © 1983 by Register & Tribune Syndicate
Copyright © 1979 by Register & Tribune Syndicate

Library of Congress Catalog Card Number: 83-90789

ISBN 0-449-12835-0

Printed in Canada

First Ballantine Books Edition: December 1983
Tenth Printing: May 1990

"It isn't Grandma."

"All right, what's all this quiet about?"

"When little girls get bigger they all seem to grow out of shape like that."

"It's for the bake sale at school, but I can buy
it back if you want me to."

"I got a 98 today! Miss Johnson took my temperature."

"How can they pack such big flowers into such tiny seeds?"

"Dinner in the yard is just eating outside. For a
REAL PICNIC you hafta get in the car
and go someplace."

"They're homemade flowers from our garden."

"Dear Easter Bunny: Please bring me a large
chocolate egg filled with coconut cream, some
jelly beans, heavy on black . . ."

"Look, Mommy! An Easter bonnet."

"Mommy, why does your eggnog taste different than mine?"

"Don't worry about it. Ours won't be the only chocolate-covered tax return they'll get."

"Which do you wanna see first, Daddy? My report card, the test paper or the note from Mrs. Gallagher?"

"... then we went on the roller coaster ...
then we ate lunch . . . then we went on the
merry-go-round . . . then Dolly threw up
. . . then we came home."

"When will the flowers start climbin' up their ladder?"

"I got a gold star for attendance, Mommy,
and guess where she put it!"

"Mommy! Look what Dolly grew on her forehead!"

"Of COURSE I notice something new, Love.
It's your . . . face . . . your forehead . . .
a STAR on your forehead!"

"You might wash off the star!"

"Couldn't I stay home from school today to go
show Grandma my prize for
perfect attendance?"

"... and here's a star for you, Jeffy, for picking up your toys, and another one for eating your lunch, and ..."

"Well! How were things down in the mine today?"

"But, Mommy! I don't know how to work it."

"Why do you have this pillow over your head, Daddy?"

"My toes love sandals because they can see out."

"Oh, no! You golfed your tee."

"Daddy, why did you tell Mommy you think
they ought to do away with tipping?"

"If I pull this string will it fall apart?"

"Would you like me to show you around
our tent?"

"Look what's in our driveway! A real
live truck!"

"Is that flotsam or jetsam?"

"The morning glories are open for business."

"We've gotta do our spilling outside."

"You can answer that kind of a door without your pants."

"'Stead of 'love' let's just say 'zero'."

"I win, Daddy! I had 142, and you only had 78."

"That's a good thing about dresses. You can make a table with them."

"I wish I could fly on a trapeze so I could wear one of those little shiny silver bathing suits."

"If this one's a fork, is this one a 'THREEK'?"

"Hi, Daddy! Want some mud pizza?"

" . . . and when the flowers are born you'll be
their father."

"If you find a golf ball, it's mine."

"One peanut butter and jelly on white, and he'll have a jumbo cheeseburger, french fries and a chocolate shake."

"Are you very busy right now, Mommy?"

"I pushed most of mine downstairs."

"Let's let the rain run awhile till it warms up."

"See? It turns itself into a sliding board!"

"After this one, Daddy . . . No, wait! After
this next one . . . Hold it . . . Now!
. . . No, after the blue one . . .
OK . . . No, wait . . ."

"Will you get in bed with me, Mommy? I don't
like to sleep alone."

"Daddy gets put to bed the same time as us tonight 'cause he's going fishin' tomorrow."

"Arizona got the highest mark."

"Could you use a good hole for anything, Daddy?"

"Billy isn't going into the Army! He's going to a summer camp for a couple weeks."

" . . . and, Dolly, you can play with my robot
and I'll let Jeffy use my skateboard,
and, PJ, you can . . ."

"I was homesick for a while, but I got over it
when the bus pulled out and I couldn't
see my mom waving."

"Why do they call the teachers 'counselors'?"

"Ya mean it's not heated?"

"Even if they ARE all reruns, we're sure missin'
a lot of television."

"Wish my mom was here to make me eat this."

"If we sink, which one of us has to go down
with the ship?"

"Mommy! It's a letter from Billy, but it has 15 cents postage due. Do we want to pay it?"

"Dear Mommy and Daddy: Today we have to
write home. Love, Billy.   PS. Don't touch
this letter or you might catch my
ivy poison."

"Do I hafta know any words besides 'giddyap' and 'whoa'?"

"I just remembered — my father already HAS a wallet."

"I shoulda brought my mom's microwave oven
— it's faster!"

"Maybe our folks don't have to pay for
rainy days."

"I'm only allowed to use arrows with rubber suction tips."

"When Billy comes home from camp I don't think I'll know him — 'specially if he grew a beard."

"Please, Lord, just ONE fish? One bite?
A nibble?"

"Please, Mommy? Couldn't I stay
another week?"

"Well, well, little people, been good children
while I was away? By golly, PJ, I believe
you've put on a little height. And, you,
Jeffy my boy . . ."

"Daddy, will you fatten up my horse?"

"I'll show you some of the fish I caught at camp when we unpack my suitcase."

"That noise means it's empty, Jeffy . . .
I said, when it makes that noise it's . . .
Jeffy! . . . Jeffy? . . ."

"Jeffy's gettin' real good. His pitches only bounce once before they reach the plate."

"Wow! This world goes down a long way!"

"Why are all these black specs in my milk?"

"Why can't watermelons have one big seed like peaches?"

"We need them for bases."

"Know what? If you draw a very small
tic-tac- toe thing, it means
'number'."

"My mom's next door and she asked me to
bring over her umbrella."

"One of the things Daddy likes 'bout tennis is
the little dress Mrs. Lincicome made for
herself. I heard him tell her."

"Hurry, Mommy! Daddy's racing his engine at us!"

"Is Billy, Jeffy, PJ, Dolly or your father here?"

"We better give Daddy more to eat. I just beat him arm-wrestling."

"I'm makin' her food and her dress the same
color so if she spills any it won't show."

"PJ will be right out of the bathroom. I just heard Mommy say 'good boy!'"

"I wish you'd mow this rug, Daddy."

"Put some lather on mine, too, please."

"I'm givin' Mommy a spiritual bouquet and usin' my money to get a catcher's mitt."

"I think you'd do better if you tried NOT
singing to him."

"You'd like this story, Mommy. It has a mother in it."

"I want a lot of outside."

"Mrs. McCall is comin' to sit with us. She's the
one who always bursts into tears."

"Is that new one gonna be his real tooth?"

"It won't fly. All it does is taxi."

"I hurt my elbone!"

"On second thought, let's take a booth."

"Billy! You better hold Daddy's hand so that if an animal escapes it won't eat you!"

"I wouldn't wanna sit behind him at
the movies."

"If the chimp is the smartest of all the animals do they pay him the most money?"

"They remember even longer than mommies."

"I bet he'd be easy to ride. Look at the handlebars."

"That's a boa constrictor. He can hug you to death."

"The sign says 'Dromedaries' but they sure
look just like camels."

"Billy's saving some of his lunch to feed the
animals and that's not allowed!"

"He'd have an awful time gettin' a sweater on."

"Come back, Dolly. He's not through
looking at you."

"If he's so sly how did he get caught?"

"Jeffy went back to say goodbye to the
gorilla."

"How long till dinner, Mommy?"
"One more inning."

"I think maybe Daddy doesn't like it around
here. He's always runnin' away."

"Ever since the day you broke your arm fallin'
off your skateboard, I haven't been
able to find mine."

"You'll have to go someplace else to blow bubbles."

"Daddy's gonna be real surprised when he comes back from downtown. We're washing his license plates for him."

"Babies grow up to be kids after a couple of whiles."

"I think this scale is slow."

"Mommy said rain makes things grow, so I put
PJ out there."

"Where's Mommy?"
"In the house getting control of herself."

". . . a bottle cap, half a scissors, a golf ball, a
doll's arm, a battery, a piece of a yo-yo . . .
this stuff all belongs in Mommy's
junk drawer!"

"Starting now all the months end with 'brr'
because it's getting colder."

"How many 'Back to School' days till Christmas?"

"Can I skip my homework, Mommy? The
teachers went on strike."

"Could you come back later? Mommy's tryin'
to give me a bath."

Adapted by Jenny Miglis

At the edge of the Great Barrier Reef in Australia lived a clownfish named Marlin and his only child, Nemo.

Marlin was extraprotective of Nemo because his son was born with a "lucky" fin. It was smaller than his other one and made him an awkward swimmer.

On Nemo's first day of school, his class went on a field trip. Nemo and his new friends sneaked away to very deep waters. Soon Marlin arrived and scolded his son—in front of all his friends! Nemo was angry that his dad had embarrassed him. So he swam far out toward the bottom of a boat floating overhead and touched it!

"Nemo!" Marlin shouted, watching as a scuba diver swam up behind his son.

"Daddy! Help me!" Nemo cried as the diver scooped him up.

But before Marlin could do anything, Nemo was gone! As Marlin chased the boat that was carrying his son away, he met a friendly fish named Dory. She was very forgetful, but she was happy to help Marlin.

Together, Marlin and Dory met Bruce, Anchor, and Chum—a group of sharks having a party. Even though the sharks insisted they thought that fish were friends, not food, Marlin still didn't trust them.

All of a sudden, Marlin spotted a diving mask just like the one worn by the diver who had taken Nemo!

"What does this mean?" Marlin asked about the words written on the side. "I can't read human!"

Soon enough, Dory realized *she* could read human! "P. Sherman, 42 Wallaby Way, Sydney," the forgetful fish read aloud.

That's where they would find Nemo! But how would they get there?

Meanwhile, far away, a hand dropped Nemo into unfamiliar waters. As Nemo swam, he bumped into invisible walls at every turn. This was surely *not* the ocean.

Slowly, several fish emerged from behind plastic plants and greeted Nemo. They told him he was in a fish tank in a dentist's office. Then Nemo learned his fate: he was going to be given to the dentist's niece, Darla . . . who had shaken her last fish to death!

Out in the ocean, Marlin and Dory had troubles of their own. After a group of moonfish gave them directions to Sydney, the two narrowly escaped a school of jelly-fish, took a wild ride with some friendly sea turtles, got lost, and were swallowed by a whale!

The whale eventually surfaced and spouted Marlin and Dory right into Sydney Harbor. But the two fish were nearly eaten by a pelican named Gerald. Right away, Nigel, a pelican friend of the Tank Gang, overheard Marlin talking about Nemo, rescued the two fish, and flew them toward 42 Wallaby Way!

Back at the dentist's office, Gill, a moorish idol fish, had devised an escape plan.

First they had to break the filter. When the dentist, Dr. Sherman, removed the fish to clean the tank, they'd roll themselves out the window and into the harbor!

Nemo picked up a pebble and swam toward the tank filter. He had tried and failed once before, but this time, with Gill's help, he was able to stop the filter by wedging the pebble in its spinning blades.

"You did it!" cheered Gill as Nemo emerged safely.

But the Tank Gang's excitement didn't last long. The dentist installed a new filter while the fish were sleeping and ruined the plan!

Then, Dr. Sherman scooped Nemo into a net. The Tank Gang jumped in and started to swim down, forcing the net away from the dentist. But Dr. Sherman captured Nemo in a plastic bag.

Suddenly, the door opened. It was Darla! "Fishy, fishy! Fishy!" she cried.

Inside the bag, Nemo quickly decided to play dead. Everyone in the tank cheered. If the dentist flushed Nemo down the toilet, he'd travel down the plumbing to freedom!

Instead, the Tank Gang watched in horror as the dentist headed for the trash can!

At that moment, Nigel flew in through the open window, carrying Marlin and Dory in his mouth. Startled, the dentist dropped Nemo's bag. Darla picked it up just as Marlin peered out of Nigel's mouth. He saw Nemo playing dead—and feared the worst.

Dr. Sherman pushed Nigel back outside and shut the window. Marlin did not get a chance to see that Nemo was all right. He also did not see Gill launch himself out of the tank and onto Darla's head!

Darla dropped Nemo's bag onto a dental mirror. The bag popped! Nemo fell out onto the mirror. Gill landed next to him and whacked the mirror with his tail, catapulting Nemo into the spit sink . . . and down the drain!

Back in the harbor, Nigel dropped Dory and Marlin into the sea. Marlin was heart-broken . . . until, at last, Nemo found him.

But their happiness was short-lived. Before their eyes, a fishing net swept Dory up with a school of groupers!

Remembering how the Tank Gang jumped into the dentist's net to help save him, Nemo swam into the large fishing net. "Swim down!" he yelled.

"Nemo, no!" Marlin cried.

"I can do it!" Nemo assured him.

Proudly, Marlin agreed. "I know you can, son."

Soon the fish had broken through the net. Nemo had saved the day!

Weeks later, Marlin and Nemo raced to school. Nemo was so excited to see his friends and teacher. He hurried off to say hello, but all of a sudden he stopped, turned around, and headed back to Marlin.

"Love ya, Dad," he said. And he gave him a big hug.